ALSO BY GILLIAN CONOLEY

Woman Speaking Inside Film Noir [1984]

Some Gangster Pain [1987]

Tall Stranger [1991]

Beckon [1996]

Lovers in the Used World [2001]

Fatherless Afternoon [2004]

PROFANE HALO

GILLIAN CONOLEY

Profane Halo

VERSE PRESS AMHERST, MASSACHUSETTS

Published by Verse Press

Copyright © 2005 by Gillian Conoley

Design and composition by Quemadura

Library of Congress Cataloging-in-Publication Data
Conoley, Gillian, 1955–
Profane halo : poems / Gillian Conoley.– 1st ed.
p. cm.
ISBN 0-9746353-2-4 (pbk. : alk. paper)
I. Title.
PS3553.O5144P76 2005
811'.54—dc22
2004021045

Available to the trade through Consortium Book Sales
and Distribution, 1045 Westgate Drive, St. Paul, MN 55114

Printed in the United States of America

9 8 7 6 5 4 3 2 1

FIRST EDITION

CONTENTS

For my family

DOMENIC STANSBERRY

and

GILLIS STANSBERRY

CURBY CONOLEY

and

BILLIE TOM CONOLEY

and for my friends

I love and I hate
who can tell me why?

CATULLUS

. . . both necessity and contingency, those two crosses
of Western thought, have disappeared from the post
iudicium *world . . . after the judgment, animals, plants,*
things, all the elements and creatures of the world . . .
would then enjoy an incorruptible fallenness—
above them floats something like a profane halo.

GIORGIO AGAMBEN

If I were two-faced, why would I wear this one?

ABRAHAM LINCOLN

PROFANE HALO

PROFANE HALO

This was the vernal   the unworldly human

       the most elegant car in the train.

A faithful and anonymous band of huntsmen,

a runner of red carpet

spotted with pheasants

on which an origin, a cold sun shone.

These were the black shoes,

the skirt one smoothed to speak.

The unknown tongue for which I am not the master,

chiefly the messengers

circling back through the vectors as the ashes adjust,

a loner with a hat,

a loner on a cold dark street,

a man gone away for cigarettes

on an otherwise calm evening.

And the signs that said yield, and then *Sssshh*, and then

let me sweep the porch for you.

A woman's black beads scattering into order.

Girl running along outside of herself toward.

Pale hopalong.

And time scarred up to do a beauty.

Dear Sunset that was sun of now,

Near Greatness, dear tongue my Queen, dear rock solid,

how could we know that we are forerunners?

The first characters in a crowd

and yet we were outwardly quiet.

We assemble here toward the river

or wherever the horse leads us,

dear oarsman   the valleys are green,

some bodies piled

some bodies marked and burned away.

New ones just wiped of their meconium.

In the whites of the lovers   in the evenings under.

Dear human mood   dear mated world.

There, there, now.

Dear ease of vicarious place, oil in sea.

Dear ravishment of fountain

figure in the fold.

These are the beers we drink like oxygen

in hats as large as I.

The loner going door-to-door, the paint excelling

the door in cubes of prescience, durations of grey.

Here we attach the theatre of a girl

the miniature size comprehensible

the door a seed

the tree a dwarf

the hay a stack

the uncreated still.

Cool of the evening,

thine ears consider well

the uncreated still.

Huntsman in the quietened alley

in the dark-arched door.

Train long and harpiethroated.

Earth's occasional moonlessness

laying hands

on the data in the street,

under which   loose animal

the unbending pale of whose complaint   becomes the dust's surround

THE RIVER REPLACES

The river replaces, the willow drags

a horseless rider caparisoned in red

glides over the gravestones.

Velvet is the integument I'd hope for for night.

Our doors are unlonelied

in the most diaristic indulgence, Death comes unexpectedly

and so you sure better

knock, and in a magnitude of scales.

The most full-flooded four-color process awaits there when I have time "for myself"

and cannot render it.

I had to guess "this was happening" said one self to the other

who self same said as the original broke

through the dream hole of the second,

and hurled its relapse into a momentary

acquaintance who ground significance with a tired pestle

until my sleepy lover woke. I had to shade the place

just so. Heaven it's heaven said it's heaven

pure heaven the self hands heaven's print-out

across a warm booth to another:

Heaven: Example

The heaven is without description.

Put them in one and the old will rage in a canoe.

Heaven was splashes of color

tossed casually from ecstasy to mania

so seeing had to become habitual,

seeing was certain films we could not look at,

films of commingstance. Might as well

bury me 'neath the blurry white oleander

crowding the pear tree near the family house

in its unassailable wedlock: personlock: what alchemy of emotions to accompany speech

and bit o' pain.

A grave is goodbye last ditch so long see you again, adieu.

Always within earshot, actuality becomes you.

We needed the rain.

Indoors I worked like the crow, the phone rang.

I worked at it,

and the whole time I could hear you,

you didn't have to scream.

Here is a dark suit and tie.

Appearance illumines.

Please write to me on a bed of ease.

Appearance forgets it like an egotist.

Fathom thee.

TINCTURE OF PINE

I am Citizen of the wind,   I am bird-infested

Data and regret,   the clouds purl two

                              unhitch
                    [why only one head, why only

two faces]

one for noontide   one for old horse in the mire

Furious are giants arguing over maps

History lays a violence under the peacefulness,
someone goes
driving the car

Let us go

through the porchlight

to the portal: No one and her white mare,   earphones of noise

No one lends her small ear

Poetry   before its raiment   coffin

a quiet word   the day   catching on

oh Marsha, why do you paint   the slop jar

SUNDAY MORNING

Theriomorphic clouds color of sweet milk cast shade in darkest suit.

Idolatry, a man whacking at weeds

then a young girl lips to the dusty screen door

longing for the neighbor child,

leaves falling into sequence but not category.

Accidental openings of no rest, suffering she walketh along

the burning edges of the garbage bill as if into the day. Satellite

was one of those highlighted words on the spelling sheet because it contained

a double consonant, satellite to guide me, satellite to inform, to frown up at in outer space.

Seconds, minutes tocked as these, fast bug across the floor

will survive into that opening, and soul bargain

the body on its offer, eager in its youth. And extraordinary,

extraordinary was hard, smears of orange along the noun following,

blue violet haze of dusk beneath the screen door, ETC.

Who made the afternoon was a true hell-maker.

Dead, do you camp here under random oak,

a tree to pin down the entropy, leaves' drape?

Is there no covetousness enough, a flow to humanity and other such fleshpots,

accessible phones in the towers we heard ourselves reply to,

to make a winter arbor an espaliered

galaxy—the whole fabular whole

to unremain, the lawn green

and bilious, a misty absinthian sea

heaving at his feet as God queries from behind

the dry tree and into

a blue truck rumbling neutral then lurching forward

as we take that dark drive together,

in our great gravel of a thirst, God taking his first swig,

You lied about it, the hollow ambrosia, colors of horses, the double fictions of my mouth—

NATIVE

Let me see
if I can understand you as part of the architecture

though it is the architecture of the place

that keeps killing me, dream of sky that stays
perfect blue foam, dream unfurling

gone and fusing like a hand that has fallen
into place.

You are at the pond

and the beach and over the want ads

and then I have the quieter
impulse to paint
beneath envy's carriage
along eternity's mill.

Earth kicking me up in the form of the human,

and taking the meaning
and giving back the meaning

as the photographs do with the life.

Before rheumy eyes
before young strapping eyes.

A mystery you didn't step over
the white painted hot dog stand

dwarf autumn marigold

a gold chain to look, and look away.

To looky here lies your
empty leg, your empty leg of even gin I would give you

for just the hint of I
I essence
I nuance up the flue.

For the rheumy eyes
For the young strapping eyes.

And begin bicycling a side road in the gaping jaws of

sweet anthem that plays
but follows like murder like entropy like lassitude,

a shade, and then a plain, and then a majesty.

Abandoned on the shore

             a red towel,

             oh my automaton odalisque.

The sun and the wind and the resultant white cloud

then the car gone off in yellow traffic like a "so there"

might we have in conversation,

as in who am I   to write this, who

Who   who is speaking   most whoever-ly,

Who, you are pale

though always

you are social.

As ever,   it is water from a spring

to walk with you

NEW

I says oh Jesus, can't I count on you people?

A zone goes   where sky's gone
what fresh hell for

burning and dodging, earth

more placid
where the state need not borrow. Have you seen the flowers on the river?

There is more to press them to, more

to compare. One has to swim through to find

this one   who had little to speak of.

This one who lay down though a motorcade went by.

Language of the west, please do run out into the ocean.

The art set crushed the tastemakers shamed Authority's myth laid out under
   a giant work light—

grid beware

the pile driving,

pile driving its two notes unevenly.

Some breeze   light rock in the kitchen   the dead crying not to be alive.

Human and elegant great structures Time glued,

one is seeing through slats as one

is ferried down Lethe, to green and neutral green, white trees, the dead Why

at the beginning of the question. One

doesn't come home one wakens

Persephone to ask, have you seen

the daughters of Memory? Paper

is ash, eternity takes tumbling bodies into its apartness

One is turning away

Zero has a glade

One is a fiction

One is slow in the death

One dies out over you,

arm back in curved light

One is arcing back

One is not a fiction

Zero has a glade

THE POX

Paleopathologists   discover   invisible balm on   3,000-year-old mummies,

like trochees   in the terrorists' letters.   And in   the Americas, covering the sores,

9 out of 10   Narraganset Indians, "They die   like rotten sheep," wrote one colonist,

when armies flee   at sunset   and deliberately fan   the flames of,   deliberately fan

this lack of I   so heaven   so no one   I know   will die.   I with skin intact

as on a cream-colored page   or a slicked pond.   When I am dead   and

go unsaid,   stop worry,   don't look   for a raft of trouble.   A sister steps back

into her vector.   Word comes and we eat   at the fugue of it,   on the morning porch

the sun's   public bath of social space—   what if the poems preserve us?

So no one I know will die,   that's my   sister in

the sundown flame, in the feeling of

intimacy that is mineral,   bitter asteroid,

"for I have the warmth
of the sun
within me at night."

LINCOLNESQUE

Peace does not appear so distant as it did.
Nor legs so long

as if to ask,
is this a marriage or an allegory?

Enter do you want
          a Negro woman for a slave
          or a wife?

"I could just leave her alone."

War next   next/next
over in less than a week, sure thing most excellent
chief, high hat with no man in, death close-walking—

Enter Captain Lilac
brought the enemy
down
but
enemy
resurrected
through
dooryard
last—

a laughingstock, the green states,
who once had his
"persuasion, kind, unassuming persuasion."

*

One spiritualist, two spiritualists, three spiritualists,

four

dust off   black topcoat of history,
lilacs, lilacs, you and me,
we always got the histamine.

Sparrows nest
near the eyes, flee bearded Death,
concrete example:
"I am not reading. I am studying law."

Enter
        "a specious and fantastic
        arrangement of words,
        by which a man can prove
        a horse chestnut to be
        a chestnut horse."

*

Money to make rich sound
in school children's pockets,

money to know all their addresses, ordinary terrors
to keep under one's hat, muy tired.

Does poetry matter?

A cloud clearly seen is stranger than country, mystic chords and patriot graves, 'copter guard.

If Colossus could have sat down, I bet he would.

Free verse is "Ladies and Gentlemen: I appear before you merely for the purpose of
        greeting you, saying a few words and bidding you farewell.

        I have no speech
        to make, and no sufficient time to make one if I had; nor have I the strength

        to repeat a speech, at all the places at which I stop. I have come to see you
        and allow you to see me (Applause)

Enter the lawn from the rear,   grey/green, windless, eerie.
Unsifted birds layered low

lift to the oracle's ear, whippoorwill intoning over rio. (Great head above crowd,
brow in the cirrus, that's you,

spoken man)
Imagination to state:

concrete
over the dead, piled-high.
Shadow returns the sight
to wonder.

        and now I believe I have really made my speech and am
        ready to bid you farewell when the cars move on."

THIS LAND IS MY LAND

Her bosslady trousseau was crepuscular.

        Her remarks half-uttered

the documentary sound of the day.

Traffic salted   the nothing-happening parts,

           the whole had been

                  the whoever-you-are,

frozen, or instamatic,

the rise/fall   orbit,   some kind of

           guide figure at the window,

a silence tangled there.

A rim painting over the sun

in which

history would like to do a little unwriting, futurally.

History writing,

spare me.
I am afraid I will die like this,
a human face, of late.

No one understands
the writing.

The words keep saying

                    is that

our wordy bride?   Cancel and begin,

                    oh no,

                                        she is a dark contemplative.

The Victorian was once a farmhouse.

She was in the task of her biography.

Attention's fan.

In a gorgeous relativity

                a bit like reading the markers

                  in a botanical garden,

               California floats its prisons in the sea.

INELEGANT MOTHERLESS CHILD

Inelegant motherless child appears

actually on the impenetrable roadsides

Wind, shack   and roadside   Flag

lifting abstraction

lifting gravel from abstraction: pretty wild.

Wild that this   stays America, episodic are the genuflections.

You can pay
to pay attention. It is impossible

though
inelegant being: I see you plainly in the alley.   Outside.

My atrocity acquaints your atrocity
we're sitting on a stoop.

The American People
stopping to drink juice at the impenetrable roadsides.

The shore lapping in

The boatman appearing
as a guide figure in a dream,

"I can get you to Jersey."

I don't know about you,
but I want to be here.

This is the life

My imaginary thumb

in the air
to your imaginary thumb

we are both shot in the back with an arrow.

This is the life,

how it feels inside you

                civic   unruly

neither nor, nary

the old haunts

you are paid to represent

murmurous then

piercingly settled

exhaustion of the mind

I see you plainly in the alley

stick-figured

drawing

scratched among dim shapes into the

back of a chair

A LITTLE MORE RED SUN
ON THE HUMAN

A little more red sun on the human   Church program spiked to the tree

There where the child carved   Grown to the father

Daughter in the grassy lot   sky pink-streaked in raincord   Forgive

my fallen corporeality   Once I was the first germ of life

afloat in the swampy gale   Water drop, come roll away the stone,   a polaroid I pan

The world is terrifying   The land covers up

The land says to itself its eternal doubt   Green trees

are bending, tombstones

are bursting,   a boy laughs   in lag time

Aphoristic   ferryman   The community's

leafy vernacular   meaning all life

is unfinished   as the grass

grows back   The mourners bow   every so often   over the human

The river's candor   a life sentence

Hazy,   launched, stopped

Vision this honeyed outline

The shapes   suggest

it is late   afternoon   Did you   know it too

FATHERLESS AFTERNOON

Fatherless afternoon, very untitled death,

partial the anatomically endowed
tree burl that gathered many before it

along the hike the country road glorifies the human gait

the human gait developed over berries
harsh and crude

then perfected in the lunar shafts I sleep for—
I was in the life class

wanting to copy copy copy it as becries the scrivener,

the inability
of white birch
grazing the picket fence,

yellow smearing blue across the palette, white spackled

into sky over river
over upside down chair bobbing up
from the river

it is all waking up only to feel like a freak.

Do not simplify
any whole paradisiacal tale,

river held and rolled
against the small divisions,

most minute cloud displacements
please extend sunfallen hours.

Thousand words,
don't eat this.

*

Gray suit in the shape of the drapes there   busy one with texture

figure through flowered walls with open unexpressed lips

you are the big picture, my eyes to foliate later.

Window at rest now dusty in its corners, no one calling

as the lowering pink clouds
surround the motel

       ecstasy

ecstatic the sparrows
in bursts in trees
above the Western American fence.

And fatherless afternoon I spend you,

big gold watch and chain
big gold watch and chain

Dingy pool of sunlight
the white mule drinking there

Lucky stag in a waterfall

lucky stag

washing perfume from your moonlit shirts
Tide brings the one who loves you

Tide pulling the world

but you must not attach

*

God please drive slow

Contain no voice   presentable
contain

no sun   bleaching the roof,

throning   deepshaded   eden

No failure to love

longevity of

no   failure to love

the strain in every bird

fantails   scattering wind and dirt

small blue worm   on the half-eaten map

must not attach

Turning the mobile, handling
the long black snake,

thorn and crown

sky weirds
the empty lot

there is work to be done

drive slow

grave bride
with a black boutonniere, shorebird on the roof

do you feel a little displaced   so high
over the underwater lawn.

*

Orchids
snag on one's bodice, pearls abide,

still water

stewing   tangled vine,   country gate   do not attach.

The guide figures
go psalming,   patching

the chants,
secrets of mine flesh is heir to.

Census returns
of California

census returns of California
fail to indicate

the ocean has a sunlit zone, a twilight zone, a deep ocean, and abyss.

It is a world of complete darkness, bitter cold, and crushing pressure.

Extraordinary

creatures who live here,
          do we say after this is all over,

you climb the stairs of a big white farmhouse
where love inclines?

Wild roses on the fence existing,

robust with something in the human makeup,

land of shades, trembling

of sea

PAINTERLY, EPIGEAN, DREAM'S HANGOVER

A griever in a party hat
    come to lay like a corpse
    before the weeper.

Stifle me not with the opposite.

Witness the gaiety of red socks,
    I have always been
    comic to you.

Let me entertain the yellow leaves
from white birch,

let me

before I die before I die

walk
as if for the first time
    upright into the depth perception

so that I begin to shade the place.

I am loving

variously

the far lateral
        of sidewalk
        the rough sequences

of getting somewhere.

Shall we go

home now,

a little preoccupied?

If you flirt with height
        with an appetite for distance
        you will get
        exposure:
        the brain senses the body
        is too far
        off the ground
        and shuts down
        such convexities.

As interstate widens
vowels shorten

        the farther north you go.

Leaves dip into an altogether
        other climate

the houses hurt the activity maligns the letters fade over the pilot light.

As before but with the senses disarrayed at what one can say.

It's bewildering but I can get you out of storage.

On the last five evenings of a life the newspaper still read
is this necessary?
We are way beyond the elucidative stage.

To set forth thy other foot, to know of one's errand.

Oranged
sunset,

the melodies run counter.

Not known   not done

a form occurs
                    occurs
creation

attaches more world

TWO (WRITERS) ONE (ROOF)

Come space   come solitude   appearing only when

one must collect

one's countenance before a social occasion.

Is that what took your face between

low summer of the West

my paragraph of wind?

Here are a few

inked

awe flowers

for you

to color in.

Dearest.

Let us begin again.

                              my whole career   awaits!

                              O Buccaneer   in mildest sun

                                                  we slug a beer

my God frontier

the newly neutered kitchen

(there will be blood
and the dead lying at a crazy angle
on the floor)

We neutered the kitchen?
We sup the fill of it

Luckydogsluckydogsluckydogs, , , ,

totality taking some twilight ease on a small patio.

"He was a smallish man, in his middle thirties,
but in spite of the stains on his trousers, he wore them with an air."

The humor of being
vs.
eyes full of sleep
eyes sewn shut, .

no one hands a form
to complete the story.

Use "administrator" for boss
use "want" instead of need
And you
are as far
as Cho-fu-sa.

If I finish the book,
I will

take questions

though I would rather

                sleep on the bed of the page you turn

without the paper
                                intervening—

World cornice:

        Greeks performing decathlon so often in the nude,
                  and to such large crowds,

helped bring
the debris of the acropolis ·
into the European combine.

"'Wanted'" posters of Communist regime
a huge hit in Prague art scene:

Gallery of "Established Nomenklatura"
subtitled "Little Whores"
took two floors and
32 mug shots

                                        we are

                                                swept down

                                        by pressure hoses

each sound is an Easter

                                        And Passover,
                                        too, say it
                                        again, Zukofsky

The most difficult moment to endure
is not such a long Lethe from here.

Vibratory electrons flicker on with night

sulfurically
as the neighborhood subsides
into void,

the past goes creeping and flying.

Jehovah's warlords   slow in air-conditioned cars

Knock   knock

Hazel Motes keeps them   in barbed wire.

Like me they seem to want speech
for its own
sake?

To enter a stranger's kitchen
for coffee for the afterlife—

slim black silhouette against white wall
Bible under arm

to not mind the distance one sits at—
to fold at last one's hands.

All sound is cut
asunder, and this
becomes
companionable.

Untrammelled
breath
in Druids in trees
in America's
pell-mell
world
happening,
whatever
is
around

in the
33/100 of a second
in which
the vowel

arrives
east having come
west.

Wishbone: I don't need it in writing

Though there you are just now in your bare feet stepping side of the barnacles.

You do not
say this to me
yet I hear you

BIRDMAN

I feel this tragic figure sitting on me

as stars dot to dot over the water that is potable.

As shoeblack in the hair will defoliate the scalp.

As lyric, lyric cries the verb, speaking of the thing.

(As the lawyer looks around for an ashtray.)

The ferry's arc   the ferry's lamp

the inchoate sumac   the inchoate sumac's blonde wig

tossed casually now above the rocks.

City as the merciful end of perspective,

city as.

He said   may we talk briefly so that God can be glimpsed

and alongside human conversation.

Heron.   Hilarity.   Time,

hilarious white spoonbill that cannot be held in the mind.

Erotic ripple marks on shore

failing to prove one's presence,

my halting attempt in the gusting spray.

Yes, sir.   Yellow pine.

Some are more released by words. For some hell *is* other people.

He wears a green eyeshade cap, like an aging umpire,

in January 1943 issue of *American Canary*.

Title: "I Wonder."

He spoke for the pillars, the bars, the sea air, the perpendicular pronoun,

the little gods running around the rocks with small black cameras.

Sometimes I too feel like a motherless

says the lawyer,

neural damage, agrees

the doctor, each to each and in their horrible penmanship.

And nature does not abhor.

Once I was a House Sparrow

now I am a Yellow Hammer

COMMON COAT PATTERNS
OF THE TIGER HORSE

(foal) A chestnut few-spot or homozygous Leopard

Bay peacock spotted Leopard

A more common type of Leopard spotting, a transient perfection

Bay varnish roan with mask and spots, the limpid mirror of

Chestnut varnish roan with blanket from the withers back,
bald face, left/right rear
+ right front stockings, once

Bay with white spots over entire
body, frosted blanket on

hips' blaze, rear left
and right stockings, it is not realism why the seeing think the blind imagine vision

Bay Snowflake roan with star and left and right rear
socks, spur and crest

be in time with body, slit of abandon
on down to toes, the border forest,

buckskin with blanket over back,
hips with brown spots, half world

(Not all striped hooves belong
to the Lp gene [leopard spotting gene]   Roan

with ghost face, we are good, we are very good for nothing, Mallarmé's astral milk

Red leopard, brown mask,
I know someone well enough to order for them in a café

Black bay leopard, no mask, no stockings, I know just
what they want, I speak the patois of that skill

Red leopard, brown mask, white rear stockings,
more mist maintaining composure

with no thought for the future, and figurative, and old visions,
no history, the Furies

Black leopard, no mask, no stockings, to the Future
to the Future Past to Now,

Chestnut varnish, with only sights to see,

no more to do or tell

ARCADE

When the genius stick flashes descent in the dark of dark matter over earth's six billion

it is like knowing you are tucked
safely inside a movie, and the heroine is climbing red tide, riptide—between

one spectacle and another

and something good is about to happen

HELLO DUST REPLACING WHERE YOU WERE—

Pastel ticket,
you are an autoportrait

The Absolutes go ideomotoring

And hours do we burn
on shore

where we woo optic waves
of three damp Kingfishers on rusted car's

prismatic roof—
I love a gone plain

Meadows breathing with difficulty

Ermine Realms of Doubt
Who Never Fears April of Meaning

Or a long shade over a grave

Apple cut into stars
is blind seed

(is young Darwin sleeping under the Redeemer)

(a third come to visit most holy)

shaped where the clouds disperse I am always with you

on a frontier punctuated with urns we keep

a small garden under middle willow

my hand in the hand

your hand gardens

a real sky drizzling over a man in black overcoat

on cobbled street
logic leaves us

between picture and dream

look at things   this angle

shattered glass archway   sky haunts
phrase   before phrase   begins to pause

ONE

One
privately
owned airplane
disappearing into
business
you could fancy it
the most melancholy sound in nature

a place to sprint from the center

new
in scale the screen

making memory the eye following

the screen   more Chaplinesque
            than ever

the picture pouring soot on you/   Your morning coffee of ash

shoes on the detached stair
more-than-time   breaking the heavenly scape

What
should we tell the citizen?

"I think
all my guys
are dead"

The citizen softly projected toward the building

That was something did you

                                  see that?

Who
picks up
a shovel

When there is nothing to contain
                        you

minister to
doctor to

Night wounds, let me introduce you
to the day wounds

flag off a yacht

over a plank in reason
flaps back

flapping back

THE GARDEN

The world news wants more than a little exile, is it that you were trying
to lie down too much in red dirt with dusk?

Sirens mean the garden is partially thumbed out.

And I have a smudge on my cheek, the bird is being incoherent with me.

The last rite, the third
witness, more news lurking over the waiting dinner.

Repositional clouds reveal less and less a blank dossier.

No rest for you, My Wicked.

MY ELECTED OFFICIALS ARE FALLING INTO HISTORICAL MOMENTS

In the stray world I drive my tractorlike car
through the capital
fain I would read the wall

in the roadside toilets light anoints a sky
prayers in my gullet like a wounded soldier
stone asleep on a cold floor

at the postal station I awake and out of the p.o. boxes pop all these penises
each with a pink ribbon

just like yesterday, says a voice I am descended from
gathering watercress beside the river to make these delicate sandwiches
at streetcorners' deserted babel manifesto and other sounds of death

NEXT AND THE CORNER

And so it was,

in such a way, like aging into my days

I had come to resemble

the dead movie house on Mission
called the El Capitán.

Three figures
at the gates of the gully,

gold March sun tinged with shadow—
as the other cars kept pulling away—

across the plain—in the hillside,

admixture of red bottle brush   and the plane overhead

three figures at the gates of the gully,

so who do tell the dead most of youth is misspent
curating a secret language,
who do tell the dead.

Fence to the fencepost,
you be lost,
you be contained.

THREE FIGURES AT THE
GATES OF THE GULLY

an airport by matchlight

no usual   links   thick the clouds

in the form

of unsayability—

for a change,

it's poetry that neglects the capital

BURNT CITY

Nitrous,   blanched,   another   hole in space   a tiny armpit   a flower

a spot of blood   on the blank document,

the tyrant and the harpy   circling the foundation,

chasing one another,   the night a color killer   the vector

twirled and shut

in the hydraulics in which night flings forward

to touch your finger

to liberty,

to feel bruised by redemption,

the plasma that constitutes,

a way to say

people ARE worth the effort

though they heat and crowd one another

in the wrong quadrant of the brain,

if we demur

breasts of a kind person

a starlike illogic

*

One stopped chugging engine
the lyric fashioning a flute

of rivercane,

Andy shot so the mylar balloons.

The multiples and multiples of Marilyn
                    ancient sources tell us

                                        pale and ruddy
                                        olden days, a city

                                            one little flap of secret longing,

                                            and eventual

                                    pockets of smart management,

                                    hot plates,   and on the third day,

                                    crème brulée   international

policy to animate, to gladden

Dug out in the ground in November

                              the undermall listening through its holes

                    *

Like giants with all our might

unmediated in one's dark apartment,

tower   from which the hair defoliates,

an I
of yore
                        as the sun

supinates, transfixes there,   red twilight

                                        like giants with all our might

high-hatted ones on pintos under sun

an imaginary   liberty

                        *

Our eyes,   cameras

delicately strapped to our heads
we could barely feel them,
a grey transfer

                  tucked into the goal,

but that part was filmed separately, and in another laboratory,

                                                        a heady wine in golden palaces

my missing one, last breath into cell phone sweet everlasting one

be still, a makeshift

                  a national infancy

makeshift
                  another national infancy

nailing something in,

                              *

hunger be luck and gangplank.

A harpy chased a dog on her embroidered pillow.

And then she blew smoke into the robocop's bosom.

World silence picture shows,

red sun under eyelids,

we have just about

had it

with reality's blazing gunplay.

Skull be dogbone, syllabary hung

like wash, sun mortal beautiful because it can destroy

historical time,

the wind, the wind martyr

*

no giantism to take the trees

a single red ribbon in a day book   a folded fan

a day a tide a day   a whipswitch that comes one way

a spoorless quietude   hell does not wish to   sip anymore   "Integrities"

can make

somebody poor

Unsullied white flowers

of form and the form of darksome cloud

pine lanes and the fresh horses who fly into them,

fly through them,   fly in

EVERY EPOCH

dreams it has been destroyed by catastrophe.

                  a mass ego only properly exists in earthquakes
and catastrophes,
                  a mass ego as in music,

the one song everyone loves.
but the violence one has to incorporate is great,

                  the joy is mighty,

                  the one song everyone loves, loved.

every epoch dreams time is a water garden in a weedy churchyard.

no Hell in your draft

there are other terrors.

                  I sleep
                  You sleep
                  He she it sleeps
                  You sleep they sleep we sleep.

the incomparable moon chapter, over mine enemy.

                  strong leader dozes off in horizon's dank corridor

                  calm nights along sensorium's riverbank.

objects freed of their utility completely unmoored.

an epoch dreams and one follows any adversary on land,

any adversary

in the bottom of the brain,

an enemy sitting across from a lover,

calmly editing a lover,

her salad a mirage.

a real world could come back to us as an epoch,

similar to a short while and a further example.

ecstatic child leaning over a pickle barrel.

a time bruise on the pickle barrel.

a few masterpieces droop, an epoch

dreams in the ruinous thereof.

every epoch dreams, and one follows.

every epoch dreams, one follows

as a figment in one setting beyond this earth even.

IT WAS THE BEGINNING OF JOY
AND THE END OF PAIN

The sewing machine had a sort of genius, high, oily and red

over that little hellion's pants.   Joy and Pain crossing legs,

then coloring in the poverty—

Are we a blue, blue whine in the restive trees?

Are we under the imprecision?

The beginning endless, ending like chasing deer out of the yard,

sphere unto sphere it takes a loyal Enthusiast
to be
Death's mother. Stag on the meadow,

mare in the river,
unwinding green river   wide rock for the resting.

The man and the woman liked to go there,
sprawled across

the warm hood of the car, a question under sky, a curve where the trees rustled.

A patch of brown hair on the white clapboard
where the deer tried to run off
scraping its side,

harsh light in the paint can,

                              weightless
     the screen door until you
heard it click shut.

She placed the shell and the action figure beside one another.
Who is king, my queen, as many tongues as there are swords.

Gone to field, weeds sway, some places are still
semi-barbarous you can make a fire under the bridge and smoke.

A headless man knows
how you saw what the saw sawed,

and there is usually enough poetry
to pass out, the day is ongoing,

you can get more material there
a rough sleeping   writ large.

I loved playing that hand harp,   large face
coming to ask   Who are you,   Where is   your precipice?

The pattern crying, the pins too many colors, surround, surround.

The pattern crying you be the master, I'll be the life,

have I been in this T-shirt all day, did I sleep in it, first did I see it this morning.

Was that you bound in sun on the step, living the life of the seasons, and loving,

I am recalling nothing of the unloving of ourselves,

did you not foreshorten into pattern one thing from its happening,

where you are slowly dying in a city,

I am born in a town.

Middling in a hive

nothing is daring to move anymore.

Sticking our feet into a template of lakes,

it is endless, endless and endless a schizy feeling walking back into your world

NOTES

"Profane Halo" takes its title from a phrase by the Italian philosopher and critic Giorgio Agamben. "Fresh hell" is Dorothy Parker. "For I have the warmth of the sun within me at night" is Milton. "This Land is My Land" is Woody Guthrie. "Lincolnesque" combines some material from several speeches and letters of Abraham Lincoln. "Sunday Morning" is for Bin Ramke. "Tincture of Pine" is for Jeff Clark. The lines "You do not / say this to me / yet I hear you" are a reversal of Louis Zukofsky's "I do not say this to you yet you hear me." "He was a smallish man, in his middle thirties, but in spite of the stain on his trousers, he wore them with an air" is Dashiell Hammett. "Every epoch dreams it has been destroyed by catastrophe" is Theodor Adorno's revision of Jules Michelet's notion that every epoch dreams the one to come.

ACKNOWLEDGMENTS

Much gratitude to the editors of the following publications where these poems previously appeared: *The American Poetry Review*, *Colorado Review*, *Conduit*, *Electronic Poetry Review*, *Fence*, *Five Fingers Review*, *How 2*, *Jacket*, *jubilat*, *Mary*, *New Review of Literature*, *Pool*, *Overland*, *Slope*, *26*, and *Verse*.

Thanks and appreciation to Sarah Roberts of the University of Iowa Center for the Book who published "Profane Halo" as a broadside. Many thanks also to Les Ferriss who published "Fatherless Afternoon" as a chapbook of Editions Ferriss.

GILLIAN CONOLEY is the author of *Lovers in the Used World*, *Beckon*, *Tall Stranger* (nominee for the National Book Critics' Circle Award), *Some Gangster Pain*, and the chapbooks *Woman Speaking Inside Film Noir* and *Fatherless Afternoon*. Winner of several Pushcart Prizes, the Jerome J. Shestack Award in Poetry, and included in *Best American Poetry*, she is Poet-in-Residence and Professor at Sonoma State University, where she is the founder and editor of *Volt*.